SIMPLY TRUSTING

CW01619816

Compiled by

B. McCALL BARBOUR

" Simply trusting every day;
Trusting through a stormy way;
Even when my faith is small,
Trusting Jesus, that is all "

Published by

B. McCALL BARBOUR

28 George IV Bridge, Edinburgh EH1 1ES, Scotland

First edition (in this style) – 1978

Reprinted May 1993

ISBN 0 7132 0027 8

Cover photo by T. C. Danson Smith

"I AM –"

Believe that He is, what He says He is;
This He will be to you:

"I WILL –"

Believe that He does what He says He does;
This you will find come true.

B.McC.B.

"The promises of God are sure if you only believe."
– *The dying words of General Booth.*

" 'TRUST' is the characteristic Old Testament word for the New Testament 'FAITH,' 'BELIEVE.' It occurs 152 times in the O.T., and is the rendering of the Hebrew words signifying *to take refuge* (*e.g.*, Ruth ii. 12); *to lean on* (*e.g.*, Psl. lvi. 3); *to roll on* (*e.g.*, Psl. xxii. 8); *to stay upon* (*e.g.*, Job xxxv. 14)." –
– *Dr. C. I. Scofield.*

Printed by Stanley L. Hunt (Printers) Ltd., Rushden, Northamptonshire

TRUSTING OUR FATHER

"The eternal God is thy refuge, and underneath are the everlasting arms"—Deut. xxxiii.27.

"WE often sink very low under the weight of sorrows. Sudden disappointments can carry us in an hour from the heights down to the very depths. Props that we leaned upon are struck away. What God means by it very often is just to bring us down to 'the everlasting arms'. . . . God often lays His hand heavily upon us, to remind us that we have got a FATHER. When my neighbour A—— broke in business, and twenty-four hours made him a bankrupt, he came home, saying to himself, 'Well, my money is gone but Jesus is left'. He did not merely come down to 'hard pan'—he came to something far more solid —to 'the everlasting arms'. When another friend laid her beautiful boy in his coffin, after the scarlet fever had done its worst, she laid her own sorrowful heart upon 'the everlasting arms'. The dear little sleeper was there already. The Shepherd had the lamb." *Rev. Theodore L. Cuyler, D.D.*

"Art thou sunk in depths of sorrow,
Where no arm can reach so low?
There is One whose arms Almighty
Reach beyond thy deepest woe,
God th' Eternal is thy refuge—
Let it still thy wild alarms;
Underneath thy deepest sorrow
Are the everlasting arms."

(*Rev. A. B. Simpson, D.D.*)

ONLY BELIEVE !

To know the origin of everything.

" In the beginning God."—Gen. i. 1.

" 'IN the beginning God.' This is something absolutely unique ; there is nothing like it anywhere else in literature. 'In the beginning God.' I could not know that by experience. I could not get to know it by the testimony of others. I can only know it on the 'Testimony of the Lord.' 'By faith we understand that the worlds were framed by the Word of God.' When ? Six thousand years ago ? Or a hundred thousand years ago ? I do not know, and I do not care. I cannot tell when human time became an inset in a Divine eternity. But I do know, by God's revelation, that 'in the beginning God' created, and so there came the beginning of the human family, and of history ; the beginning of moral issues, and of pro-creation ; the beginning of God's appointed line of descent for dominion."

—Rev. F. J. Miles.

The Outlook.

The Atheist.

" *There is no God* ! Who tells me that this span
Of petty pain and pleasure is controlled
By other than the whim-led will of man.
He must be blind or fool. I cannot hold
Your dreamer's notion of a guiding hand ;
There is no God Whom I can understand.

The Agnostic.

I do not know ; there may be One above
Who sees the strange enigma of our life,
And wisely holds its key—perhaps in love—
Who over-rules our struggle, knows our strife ;
But it is all conjecture still, to me ;
I will believe when I can clearly see.

The Christian.

I know whom I believe. The questions rise—
The problems are not few—but I have seen
The vision far transcending all surmise—
A love that plans, a strength on which I lean ;
My Master rules, for *faith* has told me so,
I know HIM Whom *I have believed* ! I know ! "

(*Laura Rae Mills.*)

FAITH IN THE UNSEEABLE

"Have faith in God"—Mark xi.22.

"THE life of faith ever begins as that of 'the Father of the Faithful' began, with the solemn recognition of a divine will which separates. Further, Abram saw plainly what he had to leave, but not what he was to win. He had to make a venture of faith, for 'the land that I will shew thee' was undefined. Certainly it was somewhere, but where was it? He had to fling away substance for what seemed shadow to all but the eye of faith, as we all have to do. The familiar, undeniable good of the present has to be waived in favour of what 'common sense' calls a misty possibility in the future. To part with solid acres and get nothing but hopes of an inheritance in the skies, looks like insanity, and is the only true wisdom. 'Get thee out' is plain; 'the land that I will shew thee,' looks like the doubtful outlines seen from afar at sea, which may be but clouds."

Rev. Alexander Maclaren, D.D.

"I cannot read His future plans;
  But this I know—
I have the smiling of His face,
And all the refuge of His grace,
  While here below.

Enough! this covers all my wants,
  And so I rest!
For what I cannot, He can see,
And in His care I saved shall be,
  For ever blest."

(*Rev. J. Parker.*)

ONLY BELIEVE !

To know THE WAY to God.

"I am The Way, The Truth, and The Life. No man cometh unto the Father but by Me."—John xiv. 6.

"Believe Me that I am in the Father, and the Father in Me."—John xiv. 11.

"CHRIST IS 'THE WAY,'—the way to heaven and peace with God. He is not only the Guide, and Teacher, and Law-giver like Moses ; He is Himself the door, the ladder, and the road, through Whom we must draw near to God. . . . 'No man,' He declares, 'No man cometh unto the Father, but by Me.' . . .

It avails nothing that a man is clever, learned, highly gifted, amiable, charitable, kind-hearted, and zealous about some sort of religion. All this will not save his soul, if he does not draw near to God by Christ's atonement, and make use of God's own Son as his Mediator and Saviour. God is so holy that all men are guilty and debtors in His sight. Sin is so sinful that no mortal man can make satisfaction for it. There must be a Mediator, a ransom-payer, a redeemer, between ourselves and God, or else we can never be saved. There is only one door, one bridge, one ladder, between earth and heaven—the crucified Son of God. Whosoever will enter in by that door may be saved, but to him who refuses to use that door the Bible holds out no hope at all. 'Without shedding of blood there is no remission' (Heb. ix. 22).

Let us beware, if we love life, of supposing that mere earnestness will take a man to heaven, though he know nothing of Christ. The idea is a deadly and ruinous error. Sincerity will never wipe away our sins. It is not true that every man will be saved by his own religion, no matter what he believes, provided he is diligent and sincere. We must not pretend to be wiser than God. Christ has said, and Christ will stand to it, 'No man cometh unto the Father but by Me.' 'I AM THE WAY.'

Forever let us grasp and hold fast these truths. To use Christ daily as the Way,—to believe Christ daily as the Truth,—to live on Christ daily as the Life,—this is to be a well-informed, a thoroughly furnished, and an established Christian."—*Bishop J. C. Ryle.*

"Thou art the Way, by Thee alone
From sin and death we flee,
And he who would the Father seek,
Must seek HIM, Lord, through Thee."

TRUSTING HIS FAITHFULNESS

"Hope thou in God"—Psalm xlii.11.

"OH, remember this—there is never a time when we may not hope in God. Whatever our necessities, however great our difficulties, and though, to all appearance, help is impossible, yet our business is to hope in God. And it will be found that it is not in vain; in the Lord's own time help will come.

Oh, the hundreds, yea, the thousands of times that I have found it thus within the past seventy years and four months! When it seemed impossible that help could come, help did come, for God has His own resources, and these resources may be counted by hundreds, by thousands. He is not confined to this thing or that thing, or to twenty things. In ten thousand different ways, and at ten thousand different times, God may help us. Our business is to spread our case before the Lord, in child-like simplicity, to pour out all our heart before God and tell Him.

Whilst we have often been brought low, yea, so low that we have not had even as much as a single penny left, or so as to have the last bread on the table, and not so much money as was needed to buy another loaf, yet never have we had to sit down to a meal without our good Lord having provided nourishing food for us. I am bound to state this, and I do it with pleasure. My Master has been a kind Master to me; and if I had to choose this day again as to the way of living, the Lord giving me grace, I would not choose differently."

George Müller.

"Dear restless heart, be still, don't fret and worry so;
God has a thousand ways, His love and help to show;
Just trust, and trust, and trust, until His will you know."

(*Edith Willis Linn.*)

ONLY BELIEVE !

To please God.

" Without faith it is impossible to please Him."—Heb. xi. 6.

" Faith cometh by hearing, and hearing by the Word of God."—Rom. x. 17.

" NOW, it is true that faith plays a supreme part in the Christian life, 'for by grace are ye saved through faith' (Ep. ii. 8). The Christian does not claim to know everything. There is the necessity of being *willing to believe*. Christ invited investigation of His Gospel. He flung out a challenge that if any man is willing to do God's will, he shall know of the doctrine.

Faith is not sight, and faith is not feeling. If we demand to see when God asks us to *believe*, we are not believing ; we are faithless. But after we have received Christ by faith, we ought to get assurance of salvation.

We see, then, that the Christian trusts in simple faith without actual sight on certain points. But he also knows some things because of the teachings of the Spirit. ' As it is written, Eye hath not seen, nor ear heard, neither have entered into the heart of man, the things which God hath prepared for them that love Him. But God hath revealed them unto us by His Spirit. . . . Now we have received . . . the Spirit which is of God, that we might know the things that are freely given to us of God. Which things also we speak . . . but the natural man receiveth not the things of the Spirit of God, . . . neither can he know them, because they are spiritually discerned.'

The recipe is so simple that its very simplicity will cause some to despise it. Dr. R. A. Torrey once said that the verse in the Bible that had most profoundly influenced him was Rom. x. 17. ' So then faith cometh by hearing, and hearing by the Word of God.' ' For a long time,' he added, ' I had been trying to develop my faith. I had listened to learned discourses about it, and talked to older Christians, before it came home to me that right in my Bible, in that verse, was the secret of faith.' "
—*Victor Arundel, in " The Moody Monthly."*

" Once I thought I walked with Jesus,
But such changeful moods I had :
Sometimes trusting, sometimes doubting,
Sometimes joyful, sometimes sad.

But He called me closer to Him,
Bade my doubting tremors cease :
And when I had *fully trusted*,
Filled my soul with perfect peace."

MAKING OUR CHOICE

"Consider the lilies . . . how they grow"—Matt. vi.28,29.

"PREFER not the outward show to the path of faith. The lilies, those emblems of simple faith in God, were better clothed than Solomon, and he who, like the lilies, lives by faith, as Bunyan puts it, 'lives a merrier life, and wears more of that herb called heartsease in his bosom than he that is clad in silk and velvet'. All the world can give is a poor exchange for peace with God and contentment of heart (Phil. iv. 11). So, do not let us envy Solomon his big show, for it cost him his soul. Even his wisdom, being the wisdom of this world, did not avail to save him. We are many times warned that wisdom puffeth up; is foolishness with God, and serves to keep men back from God, where it exists without the heart subjection to the revelation of God, that alone can give it any value. The wisdom that is from above is alone really wise."

George Goodman.

"I would not ask for earthly store—
Thou wilt my need supply;
But I would covet, more and more,
The clear and single eye,
To see my duty face to face,
And trust Thee, Lord, for daily grace.

Then shall my heart keep singing,
While to the cross I cling;
For rest is sweet at Jesus' feet,
While homeward faith keeps winging."

(*Dr. J. J. Maxfield.*)

ONLY BELIEVE !

To do the work of God.

" What shall we do, that we might work the works of God ? Jesus answered and said unto them, This is the work of God, that ye believe on Him Whom He hath sent." —John vi. 28, 29.

"WHEN our Lord bade his hearers 'labour for the meat which endureth to eternal life,' they immediately began to think of works to be done, and a goodness of their own to be established. 'What shall we do, that we might work the works of God ?' Doing, doing, doing, was their only idea of the way to heaven. . . . Taught by our Lord Jesus Christ Himself, one might have expected a greater readiness to *believe.* But, alas ! there are no limits to man's dulness, prejudice, and unbelief, in spiritual matters. . . . Note the high honour Christ puts on *faith in Himself.* 'This is the work of God, that ye *believe* on Him Whom He hath sent' —a truly striking and remarkable expression ! If any two things are put in strong contrast in the New Testament, they are faith and works. Not working, but *believing,*—not of works, but through *faith,* are words familiar to all careful Bible-readers. Yet here the great Head of the Church declares that *believing* on Him is the highest and greatest of all 'works' ! It is 'the work of God.'

Till a man *believes* on Jesus, and rests on Jesus as a lost sinner, he is nothing. Faith in our Lord Himself is that act of the soul which specially pleases God. When the Father sees a sinner casting aside his own righteousness, and simply trusting in His dear Son, He is well pleased. Without such faith it is impossible to please God. . . . Let all who know anything of true faith thank God and rejoice. Blessed are they that believe ! It is an attainment which many of the wise of this world have never yet reached. We may feel ourselves poor, weak sinners. But do we *believe* ?—We may fail and come short in many things. But do we *believe* ?—He that has learned to feel his sins, and to trust Christ as a Saviour, has learned the two hardest and greatest lessons in Christianity. He has been in the best of schools. He has been taught by the Holy Ghost."—*Bishop J. C. Ryle.*

" Weary, working, burdened one,
Wherefore toil you so ?
Cease your doing ; all was done
Long, long ago."

RESTING ON CERTAINTIES

"I know Him whom I have believed, and am persuaded that He is able to keep that which I have committed unto Him against that day"—II Tim. i.12.

"ALL the biographers of Michael Faraday agree that he was the most transparently honest soul that the realm of science has ever known. He moved for fifty years amidst the speculations of science, whilst, in his soul, the certainties that cannot be shaken were singing their deathless song. . . . In life, as in death, he rested his soul upon certainties. And, if you ask what the certainties were, his biographers will tell you they were three:

First, he trusted implicitly in His Father's Love.

Second, he trusted implicitly in the Redeeming Work of his Saviour.

Third, he trusted implicitly in the Written Word.

. . . . . .

In him the simplicities were always stronger than the sublimities; the child outlived the sage. As he lay dying they tried to interview the professor, but it was the little child in him that answered them. 'What are your speculations?' they inquired. 'Speculations?' he asked, in wondering surprise. 'Speculations? I have none! I am resting on certainties. I know whom I have believed, and am persuaded that He is able to keep that which I have committed unto Him against that day.' And, revelling like a little child in those cloudless simplicities, his great soul passed away. . . . Happy the heads that, in the soul's last straits, find themselves pillowed serenely there!" *Dr. F. W. Boreham.*

"Lord, give us such faith as this,
And then, whate'er may come,
We'll taste, e'en here, the hallowed bliss
Of our eternal home!"

(*Rev. W. H. Bathurst.*)

ONLY BELIEVE !

To obtain life everlasting.

" When He (the Holy Spirit) is come, He will reprove the world of sin, . . . because they believe not on Me."— John xvi. 8, 9.

"WHAT is the greatest sin in the world? It is not intemperance; it is not lust; it is not dishonesty; it is not a thousand other things which might be mentioned. It is unbelief.

I know it, because He said Himself that the Spirit was to come to 'reprove the world of sin, and of righteousness and of judgment,' and then He said, 'Of sin, because they believe not on Me.' Unbelief makes God a liar. He has stated certain great truths in the Bible regarding the past, present, and future life of the individual. He has told us about sin, and its remedy; about His Son, and His love. Faith is giving assent to all He has stated. Unbelief is the rejection of His statements, and counting them either as if they were not worthy of credence, or not of sufficient importance to occupy our time or thought.

Unbelief is a blow at God's Word. Here great principles are stated, marvellous promises made; precious truths offered for the testing. Unbelief is indifference, a sneer, a contemptuous treatment of God's message. In other words, unbelief is rejection. But the Bible is the standard of judgment, and the Book we reject, whatever may be the spirit of our rejection, will one day rise to judge us.

Unbelief is an arraignment of Jesus Christ, and an announcement, either by word, or act, or thought, that the story of the prophets, the account of the journey of the wise men to the star-marked cradle, of His incomparable youth, as well as the story of His great life, and the record of His death and resurrection, are not true, or, at least, are not worth our thought. Unbelief is something more: it is declining to believe in the object of His life, and the reason of His death—refusing to believe in the Lord Himself. When the day of judgment dawns, the question of questions will be, not 'Were you drunken, or impure?' but 'What did you do with Jesus?' and your answer to this question will determine your position before God there, as your relation to Him in this life determined it here."—*Rev. J. Wilbur Chapman, D.D.*

**" What will you do with Jesus?
Neutral you cannot be;
Some day your heart will be asking,
'What will He do with me?' "**

IMPLICITLY TRUSTING

"Thou wilt keep him in perfect peace, whose mind is stayed on Thee; because he trusteth in Thee"—Isa. xxvi.3.

"TRUST Jesus in and for everything. When a trial is past, one does so bitterly regret not having trusted Him entirely in it; and one sees that we might as well have had the joy and rest of perfect trust all along." So wrote Frances Ridley Havergal.

Throughout her life, though often in weakness and physical suffering, her overflowing heart was ever telling of her trust in the faithfulness of God. And so she sang:

"I am trusting Thee, Lord Jesus,
Trusting only Thee!
Trusting Thee for full salvation,
Great and free.
I am trusting Thee for pardon,
At Thy feet I bow;
For Thy grace and tender mercy,
Trusting now.
I am trusting Thee for cleansing,
In the crimson flood;
Trusting Thee to make me holy
By Thy blood.
I am trusting Thee, Lord Jesus,
Never let me fall!
I am trusting Thee for ever
And for all."

As it was throughout her life, so was it at its close. After a parting message to her dear ones to "Trust Jesus", clearly, though faintly, she sang:

"Jesus, I will trust Thee,
Trust Thee with my soul,
Guilty, lost, and helpless,
Thou *hast made* me whole.
There is none in heaven,
Or on earth, like Thee;
Thou hast died for sinners,
Therefore, Lord, for *me*."

Then she nestled down in the pillows, folded her hands on her breast, saying, "There, now, it is all over! Blessed rest!"

"She, being dead, yet speaketh."

ONLY BELIEVE !

To be "a Christian."

"I know Whom I have believed."—II Tim. i. 12.

"THE Christian religion stands over against all religions of forms and duties, as the religion of life and of love, as the religion of personal attachment to Christ, and glad possession of Him. Those who profess to be Christians should know Who He is Whom they profess, and should know also why and how they have come to be Christians. To acknowledge the fact of Christ in human history does not make one a Christian, neither does giving intellectual assent to His claims on the evidence supplied by the Gospels. Many do this who make no Christian profession. And attachment to a Christian Church, by any means whatever, does not make one a Christian, and is no evidence that one is such. A lady once applied to me for membership in my church, and when I asked her if she were a Christian, she hotly replied, 'That's my business !' Of course it was her business, and the tragedy was that she was not attending to it. . . . Yes, the salvation of our souls is our personal business, and we do not attend to it by having our names put on a church roll ; indeed, our names have no right to be there until we have attended to this business. A Christian Church is not a Religious Club, but is a company of people who have an experimental knowledge of Christ, who have Him to be their Saviour, not because the Bible says that He can save, but because they know that *He has* saved them. Christianity is religion, but all religion is not Christianity. All men are religious, but all are not Christians. . . . The early disciples were called *Believers*, because they trusted the person of the Redeemer ; because 'they turned to God from idols, to serve the living and true God, and to wait for His Son from Heaven' (I Thess. i. 9-10). That is a good definition of a Christian—one who has *turned*, and now is *serving* and *waiting*. We cannot serve God acceptably until we have turned to Him, and we are not likely to look for Him, if we have neither turned nor served. It is to be feared that many are trusting to good works for their salvation, and are making *serving* a substitute for 'turning.' "—*Dr. W. Graham Scroggie.*

"I am trusting Thee, Lord Jesus,
Trusting only Thee !
Trusting Thee for full salvation,
Great and free."

A CHALLENGE TO TRUST

"I, the Lord thy God, will hold thy right hand, saying unto thee, Fear not; I will help thee"—Isa. xli.13.

"Lead me, and guide me"—Psalm xxxi.3.

"The darkness and the light are both alike to Thee"—Psalm cxxxix.12.

"IT takes the night to bring out the glory of the stars. It requires the storm-cloud to make it possible to paint the rainbow. Tribulation and affliction are only the wrapping-paper round God's priceless miracles and joys. God's dealings with us often seem, to the outward eye, dark and terrible. Faith looks deeper, and says—'This is God's secret; you look only on the outside; I look deeper and see the hidden meaning.'

Let us not become impatient with God; but understand that there are two ends to every tunnel, and that the Hand that leads us in is the same loving Hand that will lead us out, yea, and will hold our hand as we journey through." *Mrs. Chas. E. Cowman.*

"A tender child of summers three,
Seeking her little bed at night,
Paused on the dark stair timidly.
'Oh Mother! Take my hand,' said she,
'And then the dark will be light.'

We older children grope our way
From dark behind to dark before
And only when our hands we lay,
Dear Lord, in thine, the night is day,
And there is darkness nevermore.

Reach downward to the sunless days
Wherein our guides are blind as we—
And faith is small and hope delays;
Take Thou the hands of prayer we raise,
And let us feel the light of Thee!"

(*John Greenleaf Whittier.*)

ONLY BELIEVE !

To have an established life.

" Have faith in God."—Mark xi. 22.

"WITHOUT faith in God, man drifts on a stormy ocean without a pilot ; he wanders on a barren desert without a guide. There is no shipwreck so melancholy, or terrible, as the shipwreck of faith.

One of mankind's chief supports in this life is the comfort and strength which come out of faith in the Providence and the Fatherhood of God. There will always be much, on the surface at least, of life, to assail that faith, and to say, ' Where is now thy God ? ' Yet faith in the providence of God, however and whenever assailed, is a mighty defence of the soul. One of our most precious and practical beliefs is that out of the struggle with pain, temptation, and sorrow, purity and nobleness of character emerge, and that, back of all events of life, there is the plan and purpose of a wise and beneficent God. For this faith there is no possible substitute. It is either trust in the Providence of God, or life is a bitter and meaningless struggle, from darkness to darkness.

With the sinking of faith in God, communion and prayer, with all their sanctifying influence, would be impossible. It is true, sadly true, that vast multitudes of men never pray. But there is a gulf of difference between never praying and having no God to Whom to pray. Without prayer, without communion with the invisible and eternal, men are but insects crawling on the planet. . . .

The Cross is God's heartsease for troubled and sinning mankind. But, if there is no God, the light fades from the Cross, and its Divine Victim is lost in Calvary's ninth-hour darkness. There still are left some in this vexed and troubled world who *believe in God*, and who are finding joy and peace in that belief—a joy and peace which the world cannot take away."—*Rev. Clarence E. Macartney.*

" My hope is built on nothing less
Than Jesus' blood and righteousness;
I dare not trust the sweetest frame,
But wholly lean on Jesus' name."

SHARING OUR BURDEN

"Casting all your care upon Him; for He careth for you"— 1 Peter v.7.

"DEAR reader, if you know Jesus as your Saviour, beware lest Satan beguile you to believe that you have one want or care too minute for the consideration of the God of the whole earth. 'All things were made by Him and for Him.' . . .

'Casting ALL your care upon Him,' does not imply such concerns as the natural intellect may decide on as fit occasions for faith and prayer. It necessarily includes *whatsoever* can burden, or tempt, or grieve a child of that Father, who declares that the very hairs of our head are numbered. Prove the blessed truth of faith in Jesus. Give Him the first place in your heart and counsels; soon you will feel that you cannot do without Him in the least matter, and every occasion of going to Him will result in new manifestations of His love and faithfulness.

Anna Shipton in "Tell Jesus".

"Thou knowest, Lord, Thou knowest all about me,
And all the winding way my feet have trod;
And now Thou know'st I cannot go without Thee,
To guide me onward through the swelling flood.

Thou know'st my way—how lone, how dark, how cheerless,
If Thy dear hand I fail in all to see;
Bright with Thy smile of love, my heart is fearless,
When in my weakness I can lean on Thee.

Give me Thy presence! Go Thou, Lord, before me;
Make a plain path where all is rough and drear;
So let me trust Thy love that watches o'er me,
And in the shadows still believe Thee near."

(*Anna Shipton.*)

ONLY BELIEVE !

To gain victory over Self.

" I have been crucified with Christ, and it is no longer I that live, but Christ that liveth in me."—Gal. ii. 20 **(Weymouth).**

" CRUCIFIED with Christ ! See what pains the Holy Spirit takes to teach us clearly and fully the nature and privileges of the standing in which the love of God has placed us. Now, it is in the knowledge and realization of these facts, and in the practical application of them to our hearts and consciences, that ' we are renewed after the image of Him that created us,'—stablished, strengthened, settled.

The feeblest Believer in the family of God is as truly united to Christ as the strongest. He has been as fully baptized into Christ, as truly planted together with Him, *as effectually* crucified together with Christ as any other individual Believer in the family, for all are equally members of the Head. But, when we come to speak of the different degrees of knowledge, and of the enjoyment which Believers have in these great truths, and the consequent practical power they have on their lives and affections, then indeed there are vast degrees of difference ; our realization of them, and their practical influence upon our lives and characters, will ever be in proportion to our faith. The reason why we find so many Christians feeble, and sickly, and weak . . . is not that they have not been baptized into Christ, planted together with Him, and crucified with Him, but because they have so little faith, they do not live upon the Lord Jesus Christ, they do not realize and feast on and exercise their souls in the fulness given to them in the Lord Jesus Christ ; they are faint, and weak, and failing, and suffering, because they are unbelieving and distrustful ; endeavouring to do, in their own strength and from their own resources, what can only be done through the grace of the Lord Jesus Christ enabling them."—*Rev. M. Rainsford, B.A.*

" I've reckoned myself to be dead unto sin,
 And risen with Christ and now He lives within,
The life more abundant He gives unto me,
 This overflow life gives me full victory."

THE TRIAL OF FAITH

"The word of the Lord came unto him, saying, . . . Hide thyself by the brook Cherith. . . . And it came to pass, after a while, that the brook dried up"—I Kings xvii.2-3,7.

"IN the land where the bread and the water were failing fast, Elijah was led to Cherith and fed there. That is a very simple passage in the history of God's providence—a very simple illustration of the promise, 'My God shall supply all your need'. But, the second chapter of the story makes much harder reading. 'It came to pass that the brook dried up.' God sent Elijah to the brook, and it dried up. It did not prove equal to the need of the prophet. It failed. God knew it would. He meant it to fail. . . .

'The brook dried up.' This is an aspect of the divine providence that sorely perplexes our minds and tries our faith. . . . God knows that there are heavenly whispers that men cannot hear till the drought of trouble and weariness has silenced the babbling brooks of joy. And He is not satisfied until we have learned to depend, not on His gifts but upon Himself." *Rev. Percy C. Ainsworth.*

"Perchance thou, too, hast camped by such sweet waters,
And quenched with joy thy weary, parched soul's thirst;
To find, as time goes on, thy streamlet alters
From what it was at first.
Hearts that have cheered, or soothed, or blest, or strengthened;
Loves that have lavished so unstintedly;
Joys, treasured joys—have passed, as time hath lengthened
Into obscurity.

. . . . .

If thus, ah soul, the brook thy heart hath cherished
Doth fail thee now—no more thy thirst assuage—
If its once glad refreshing streams have perished,
Let HIM thy heart engage.
He will not fail, nor mock, nor disappoint thee;
His consolations change not with the years;
With oil of joy He surely will anoint thee,
And wipe away thy tears."

(*J. Danson Smith.*)

ONLY BELIEVE !

To obtain complete victory.

" This is the victory that overcometh the world, even our faith."—I John v. 4.

" EVERY true child of God is encouraged by the New Testament to expect complete victory over the world, the flesh, and the devil. . . . It is quite certain that faith is a much more effective weapon than force. We cannot overcome the world by our mass organizations, nor through any attempt to make use of the world's methods. We can only overcome as we exercise a strong and simple faith in the One Who has promised to make all grace abound unto His people.

All this is supported by what is known as the plan of salvation. We are saved by *faith*. Faith is a complete and unwavering trust in the Son of God. We dare to believe the revelation of Holy Scripture, and from beginning to end, do not hesitate to say : ' Let God be true, and every man a liar.' Without faith it is impossible to please God, and without faith it is impossible to overcome the world. Faith is an inward power which is nourished by the Holy Spirit in the fellowship of prayer. Apart from such faith—which must be renewed and strengthened moment by moment—the believer would despair as he faces the formidable adversaries that are arrayed against him.

The secret of the victorious life is to be found in the risen power of the Son of God. . . . Here, then, we touch the heart of the victorious life. It is to be found in Christ Himself. Through His shed blood we may be empowered to follow His steps, and to walk worthily of the One Who called us. There is no other way of victory. Every other attempt is doomed to disappointment and failure. The humblest child of God, who, in simplicity and in humility, *receives* the Gospel, and *believes* that Jesus is the Son of God, may discover, *through such simple faith,* the secret of the overcoming life in the power of which the world, the flesh, and the devil are defeated and overthrown."—*Life of Faith.*

**" A life of overcoming,
A life of ceaseless praise,
Be this thy blessed portion
Throughout the coming days :
The Victory was purchased
On Calvary's Cross for thee,—
Sin shall not have dominion,
The Son hath made thee free."**

(F. H. Allen.

AN ENDLESS SUFFICIENCY

"My grace is sufficient for thee"—II Cor. xii.9.

"THE other evening I was riding home after a heavy day's work; I felt very wearied and sore depressed, when swiftly, and suddenly as a lightning flash, that text came to me: 'My grace is sufficient for thee.' I reached home and looked it up in the original, and at last it came to me in this way, 'My grace is sufficient for thee', and I said, 'I should think it is, Lord', and burst out laughing. I never fully understood what the holy laughter of Abraham was till then. It seemed to make unbelief so absurd. It was as though some little fish, being very thirsty, was troubled about drinking the river dry, and Father Thames said, 'Drink away, little fish, my stream is sufficient for thee'. Or, it seemed like a little mouse in the granaries of Egypt, after the seven years of plenty, fearing it might die of famine; Joseph might say, 'Cheer up, little mouse, my granaries are sufficient for thee'. Again, I imagined a man away up yonder, in a lofty mountain, saying to himself, 'I breathe so many cubic feet of air every year, I fear I shall exhaust the oxygen in the atmosphere'. But the earth might say, 'Breathe away, O man, and fill thy lungs ever, my atmosphere is sufficient for thee'. Oh, brethren, be great believers! Little faith will bring your souls to heaven, but great faith will bring heaven to your souls." *Rev. C. H. Spurgeon.*

"If our love were but more simple,
We should take Him at His word;
And our lives would be all sunshine
In the sweetness of our Lord."

(*Faber.*)

ONLY BELIEVE !

To experience the Victory.

" Thanks be to God, Who giveth us the VICTORY through our Lord Jesus Christ."—I Cor. xv. 57.

" GOD giveth us the Victory—
O wondrous thought !
'Tis all of grace from first to last,
By Jesus wrought.
Thanks for God's Gift unspeakable—
Of His dear Son,
In Whom is the Eternal Life
On earth begun.

God giveth us the Victory—
'Tis a free gift—
Not our own effort, but His power
That doth uplift
The trusting heart to heights above,
Where Christ doth reign ;
And keeps us looking for Himself
To come again.

In Thee we triumph, Lord, in Thee
Rejoice and sing—
For all the crowns are on Thy brow,
And Thou art King.
Within our heart we Thee enthrone
Thy Name adore ;
Jesus, pre-eminent art Thou
For evermore.

God giveth us the Victory—
And day by day
He leadeth us in triumph on
By Christ alway ;
'Midst many a conflict, sorrow, loss,
Tried and cast down ;
Yet more than conquerors by His cross,
To win the crown.

God giveth us the Victory !
We take it, Lord ;
Surrendered in our helplessness
To *trust* Thy Word.—
In *faith* we would begin to praise,
Believe, then see
That Thou dost give us, here and now,
The Victory."

—*J. M. Stuart.*

WALKING BY FAITH

"By faith Abraham, when he was called to go out into a place which he should after receive for an inheritance, obeyed; and he went out, not knowing whither he went"—Heb. xi.8.

"IT is true he knew not 'whither he went', and by so much this is what is called 'a leap in the dark'; but Abraham knew two things: (1) he knew at whose bidding he was going, and (2) he knew what results were promised to his faith. . . . We are to walk by faith, not by sight. . . . Away went Abram from Ur of the Chaldees, and on his way he received a renewal of the promise. Very beautiful was this! It shewed that he was on the right road, and that God's faithfulness followed him like an angel of defence. It is so with ourselves on the journey to the better Canaan, where the upper springs never dry, and the summer lies like an infinite blessing over the whole land.

O fair Canaan! A land so near, did we but know it! Just over the river, the stream, the faint dark rill; it was a river to our youth, it is a stream to our manhood, it will be but a rill to the faith of our old age! And, as we move to it step by step, what words of love and hope are spoken to us by the Lord of that fair land! How He helps us up the steps that are long and hard; how He cheers us along the road that is flat and tedious; how He throws a robe around us when the fierce winds blow upon us in bitter cold!"

Dr. Joseph Parker.

"God holds the key of all unknown,
And I am glad;
If other hands should hold the key,
Or if He trusted it to me.
I might be sad.

The very dimness of my sight
Makes me secure;
For, groping in my misty way,
I feel His hand; I hear Him say
'My help is sure.' "

(*Rev. J. Parker.*)

ONLY BELIEVE !

To be delivered from unbelief.

" Take heed, brethren, lest there be in any of you an evil heart of unbelief, in departing from the living God."—Heb. iii. 7-19.

"UNBELIEF is the most unreasonable thing in the world. Really there is no excuse for it. There might be an excuse for not believing your minister, for it is quite possible I might be mistaken, or I might intend to deceive, or be unable to keep my promise ; but there is no excuse for not believing God. God cannot deceive, and cannot be deceived. He cannot fail from want of resources in Himself or from want of ability to keep His pledges to poor sinners. Now, from the moment when—putting aside all you are and all you have done—you take God's word concerning Christ, what He is, and what He has done, as God's free gift to the needy and to the guilty, from that moment you have an interest in Him. When you know that you have an interest in Him, then you will begin to walk in newness of life, to hate the things that Christ hates, and to hate yourself for following or being overtaken by them, and you will begin to follow the things that Christ commands, and count them, beyond measure, more precious than gold or silver. Then, you go on to realize your new standing before God, and that He no more regards you as you know yourselves, by painful experience, to be poor and weak and needy ones. Truly God does *know* us as such, but not to condemn, *only* to supply strength to meet our difficulties, and to send the Comforter to wipe away our tears. He only knows His people as tried ones, that they may be helped. He only knows them in weakness that they may be strengthened. He only knows them as exposed to danger that they may be sheltered. He only knows them as pilgrims in the wilderness that He may walk the wilderness *in them and with them*, and bring them up out of the wilderness, leaning upon their Beloved. You will find, by experience, that herein lies the secret motive and power for consecration of heart. This knowledge enables us to look upon God without fear, to contemplate a death-bed without terror, to anticipate judgment without alarm."

—*Rev. M. Rainsford, B.D.*

" My heart swells within me with thankfullest joy
For the *faith* which to me Thou hast given ;
For in all Thine amazing abundance of gifts
Thou hast no better gift short of heaven."

(*Faber.*)

OUR ALL-KNOWING GUIDE

"He knoweth the way that I take"—Job xxiii.10.

"MY Reader—Let me speak to your very inmost heart. It is by no means enough to set out cheerfully with your God on any venture of faith. Tear into smallest pieces any itinerary for the journey your imagination may have drawn up. Nothing will fall out as you expect. Your Guide will keep to no beaten road. He will lead you by yawning gulfs and under beetling cliffs, such as you never dreamt your eyes would look upon. He knows no fear, and He expects you to fear nothing whilst He is with you. The clinging hand of His child makes a desperate situation a delight to Him. A true walk with God will do more to awaken awe, wonder, and amazement in your soul than would a century of travel through the sights of earth. It is your business to learn to be peaceful and safe in God, in every situation time or eternity can develop, in this or in any other world to which He may lead you.

To take you to His 'end' by the WAY YOU KNOW would profit you little. He chooses for you a way you know NOT, that you may be compelled into a thousand intercourses with Himself, which will make the journey for ever memorable to Him and to you."

Rev. C. G. Moore.

"In Heavenly love abiding,
No change my heart shall fear,
And safe in such confiding,
For nothing changes here.
The storm may rage around me,
My heart may low be laid,
But God is round about me,
And can I be dismayed?

Wherever He may guide me,
No want shall turn me back
My Shepherd is beside me,
And nothing can I lack.
His wisdom ever waketh,
His sight is never dim—
He knows the way He taketh,
And I will walk with Him."

(*A. L. Waring.*)

ONLY BELIEVE !

To conquer unbelief practically.

" Lord, I believe ; help Thou mine unbelief."—Mark ix. 24.

"WE see in these words a vivid picture of the heart of many a true Christian. Few, indeed, are to be found among believers, in whom trust and doubt, hope and fear, do not exist side by side. Nothing is perfect in a child of God, so long as he is in the body. His knowledge, his love, and humility, are all more or less defective and mingled with corruption. And as it is with his other graces, so it is with his faith. He believes, and yet has about him a remainder of unbelief.

What shall we do with our faith ? We must *use it*. Weak, trembling, doubting, feeble as it may be, we must use it. We must not wait till it is great, perfect, and mighty, but, like the man in the case before us, turn it to account, and hope that one day it will be more strong. 'Lord,' he said, 'I believe.'

What shall we do with our unbelief ? We must *resist it*, and pray against it. We must not allow it to keep us back from Christ. We must take it to Christ, as we take all other sins and infirmities, and cry to Him for deliverance. Like the man before us, we must cry, 'Lord, help mine unbelief.' These are experimental truths. Happy are they who know something of them. Faith and unbelief, doubts and fears, are all foolishness to the natural man. But, let the true Christian study these things well, and thoroughly understand them. It is of the utmost importance to our comfort to know that a true believer may be known by his inward warfare, as well as by his inward peace"—*Bishop J. C. Ryle*.

" My faith looks up to Thee,
Thou Lamb of Calvary,
Saviour Divine :
Now hear me while I pray ;
Take all my guilt away ;
Oh, let me from this day
Be wholly Thine."

A BLESSED EXPERIENCE

"As having nothing, and yet possessing all things"—II Cor. vi.10.

"WHEN there is nothing in sight to meet our need, what shall we do? It is a good time to rejoice. There is every reason to rejoice then. A Christian man, writing a letter to a friend, tells of sore adversity, in financial stringency and uncertainty, that has come upon himself and his wife. Does he write in complaint? Far from it! 'We are surely at the Red Sea. A generous friend, who has helped hitherto, can now help no longer. Although there is no money in sight I have no anxiety—I trust God—I feel sure He cares, and knows our need. I am having the most blessed experience trusting Him. I think He wants us all to feel the same way. No doubt we need to be made to feel that we must cease from man whose breath is in his nostrils, and look directly to Him who has promised to supply. Such a blessed experience in prayer this morning! Tears of joy flowed as He assured me that we should lack no good thing.' Then he quotes the verse:

'I know my Heavenly Father knows
The storms that do my way oppose,
And He will drive the clouds away,
And turn the darkness into day,
He knows—my heavenly Father knows.'

'The future is very bright, because He is very near and has manifested his tender love so wonderfully. His resources are unlimited, and I know He will provide.' " *Extract from "Sunday School Times"*.

"When nothing whereon to lean remains,
When strongholds crumble to dust;
When nothing is sure but that God still reigns,
That is just the time to trust.

'Tis better to walk by faith than sight,
In this path of yours and mine;
And the pitch-dark night, when there's no outer light,
Is the time for faith to shine."

(*Anon.*)

ONLY BELIEVE !

To obtain assurance of forgiveness.

" I am not ashamed of the Gospel of Christ ; for it is the power of God unto salvation to every one that believeth."— Rom. i. 16.

" JESUS CHRIST is the world's only hope. It is not surprising that the world does not believe this, but it is a tragedy and a crime that in the organized Christian Church only half believe it. . . . ' Be it known unto you, therefore, men and brethren, that through this Man is preached unto you the forgiveness of sins ; and by Him *all that believe* are justified from all things, from which ye could not be justified by the Law of Moses ' (Acts xiii. 38, 39). This is the Evangel of God, because it originates in His love ; of *Christ*, because it flows from His sacrifice ; of *the Kingdom*, because it tells of government based on redemption ; of *grace*, because it is wholly unmerited by us ; of *peace*, because it makes peace between God and the sinner ; of *Salvation*, because it receives this *for all who believe* ; of *uncircumcision*, because it embraces all men, and saves apart from forms and ordinances; of *glory*, because it unfolds and magnifies the glorious God ; and it is *everlasting*, because it never loses its character or power.

It is this we are called upon to *believe* and preach. It is this which gives to the Bible its name, and makes it the Book of books. It is this which illumines the darkness of every age, and interprets for us the significance of life.

If we would have old-time results from our preaching we must declare old-time truth with old-time passion. We must *believe* that sin is a reality, that repentance is a necessity, and that regeneration is a possibility. We must *believe* in the unwearying love of God, in the sacrifice of Christ as atoning, and in the unceasing activity of the Holy Spirit. We must *believe* in the ethical inflexibility of the Godhead, and therefore in the certainty of judgment present and to come. And we must *believe* in prayer as a practical power."—*Dr. W. Graham Scroggie.*

" God loved the world of sinners lost
And ruined by the fall ;
Salvation full *at highest cost,*—
He offers free to all."

TRUSTING FOR THE IMPOSSIBLE

"Offer unto God thanksgiving; and pay thy vows unto the Most High; and call upon Me in the day of trouble: I will deliver thee, and thou shalt glorify Me"—Psalm 1.14-15.

A WELL-KNOWN evangelist relates the following incident: I first went to America many years ago, with the captain of a steamer who was one of the most devoted men I ever knew. When off the coast of Newfoundland he said to me, "Mr. Inglis, the last time I crossed here, five weeks ago, something happened which revolutionised the whole of my Christian life.

We had George Müller of Bristol on board. I had been on that bridge twenty-four hours, and never left it. George Müller came to me and said, 'Captain, I have come to tell you I must be in Quebec Saturday afternoon'. 'It is impossible,' I said. 'Very well, if your ship cannot take me, God will find some other way—I have never broken an engagement for fifty-seven years. Let us go down into the chart-room and pray.' I looked at that man of God, and thought to myself, what lunatic asylum can that man have come from—I never heard such a thing as this.

'Mr. Müller,' I said, 'do you know how dense this fog is?' 'No,' he replied, 'my eye is not on the density of the fog, but on the living God, who controls every circumstance of my life.' He knelt down and he prayed one of the most simple prayers. When he had finished, I was going to pray, but he put his hand on my shoulder, and told me not to pray. 'First, you do not believe He will, and second, I BELIEVE HE HAS, and there is no need whatever for you to pray about it.' I looked at him, and George Müller said, 'Captain, I have known my Lord for fifty-seven years, and there has never been a single day that I have failed to get an audience with the King—get up, Captain, and open the door, and you will find the fog is gone.'

I got up, and the fog was indeed gone.

On Saturday afternoon, George Müller was in Quebec for his engagement." *Selected.*

ONLY BELIEVE !

To know God.

" In the beginning God."—Gen. i. 1.

" ' IN the beginning God.' These are the first words in our Bibles. They are glorious pillars for the gateway of Truth, the sublimest introduction to the sublimest Book in the universe. They are also glorious words with which to begin a year. . . . A year begun with and for God will end with His divine benediction. Let these words be the warning and inspiration of every purpose, word, and act. ' In the beginning God.'

He is willing to take us at nothingness, and to be to us the beginning and the ending of all our life and strength; and, indeed, He cannot do anything with or for us until He gets us stripped of all our spiritual riches and possessions, and willing to begin with only God Himself. So let us receive Him, enthrone Him, glorify Him, and live for Him.

HIM FIRST, HIM MIDST, HIM LAST, HIM WITHOUT END. In all our purposes and plans, in all our endeavour and powers, in soul and body, in word and deed, let it be ' IN THE BEGINNING GOD.' "—*Rev. A. B. Simpson, D.D.*

" How can I know HIM—God ? The very word
Suggests the thought of One unseen, unheard ;
All-unperceived, above, beyond the reach
Of every means the human mind can teach.

How can I know HIM—God ? Oh, if there were
Some ' open vision ' ; something which would stir
Imagination, based on evidence !
But no—I find no prop for mental sense.

How can I know HIM—God ? Methinks I heard
A fellow-traveller speaking of ' His Word.'
I found the Book, and in its pages clear
The record of a Revelation here !

And now, I know HIM – Jesus ! Living ' Word ' !
And own Him as my Saviour and my Lord ;
Dark mazes of ' Neology ' I flee,
And find my peace, my all, O Lord, in Thee ! "

(*Pegg Spencer Palmer.*)

TRUSTING THE SAVIOUR

"Whoso trusteth in the Lord, happy is he"—Prov. xvi.20.
"O taste and see that the Lord is good: blessed (happy) is the man that trusteth in Him"—Psalm xxxiv.8.

ARE you longing for happiness? Here, then, is the divine recipe for its possession—"Trust in the Lord." Find your happiness in HIM. The Lord is the source and centre of all true and enduring happiness.

"There's love and life and lasting joy,
Lord Jesus, found in Thee."

To receive HIM as Saviour and surrender to HIM as Lord; to acknowledge HIM in all our ways as Master, is to experience truest happiness and all that makes life worth living.

In HIM we are happy about the *past*, because our sin is, by His precious blood, for ever blotted out.

In HIM we are happy in the *present* because HE is with us as our constant companion—our never-failing friend; yea, as our very life. HE is our victory over all temptation. He is with us to save us. HE meets our every need.

In HIM we are happy because our *future* is made bright with the promises of God. "Surely goodness and mercy shall follow me all the days of my life; and I will dwell in the house of the Lord for ever" (Psalm xxiii. 6).

"Blessed (happy) is the man that trusteth in the Lord, and whose hope the Lord is. For he shall be as a tree planted by the waters, and that spreadeth out her roots by the river, and shall not fear when heat cometh, but his leaf shall be green: and shall not be careful in the year of drought, neither shall cease from yielding" (Jer. xvii. 7-8, R.V.).

B. McCall Barbour.

"Just to be happy in Jesus,
And meet every fear with faith's song,
This is my daily commission,
Though everything seems to go wrong."

ONLY BELIEVE !

To enjoy Christ's Fellowship.

"That Christ may dwell in your hearts by faith."—Eph. iii. 17.

"FAITH is our power of appropriation. The pity is that we are so slow to make use of our Lord's resources! He does not force Himself upon us. Though He brings with Him gold tried in the fire that we may be enriched, and white raiment for our clothing, and eye-salve for our blindness: and though He knows how urgently we need these things, He will not force them on our acceptance. Rather, He stands and knocks, as a travelling merchant knocks at the door, who has wares to dispose of; and we need to open the door and receive the gifts which are offered, without money and without price (Rev. iii. 18-20, Isa. lv. 1-2).

Faith is our reception of the spiritual to make good the lack of the physical. It is a drawing on the Eternal for the deficiencies of our earthly pilgrimage. Probably when we look back on our present life, we shall find that our deficiencies were permitted, and even assigned, that we might be driven to avail ourselves of the fulness of the Lord Jesus (John i. 16, Eph. iii. 19). We were allowed to wander in the sultry heat, that we might know Him as the shadow of a great Rock in a weary land: we were exposed to wild tempests and storms, that we might make for alcoves and harbours in Him that we should otherwise have missed. It has been truly observed that Job's rebellious moods arose when he thought that God was afar off, but there was a difference when he realized that God was suffering *with* him. Remember that you are not divided from God by a deep chasm. He knows your sorrows. In all your affliction *He* is afflicted. We have not a High Priest Who cannot be touched with the feeling of our infirmities. When Jesus saw the sisters weeping, He not only succoured them, but entered into their distress and wept with them. Are you weary with burdens that are crushing you? Is your lot cast with them that hate peace? Is your heart oppressed with loneliness? Take Jesus into account. Don't face your difficulties alone, but meet them in the fellowship of your Saviour. *Have faith, i.e., reckon* on God. Let the Lord Christ *dwell* in your heart, and He will be responsible for all, as you reckon on Him for all."—*Rev. F. B. Meyer, D.D.*

"We thank Thee, Lord, for weary days
When desert streams were dry;
And first we learned what depth of need
Thy love could satisfy."

A CHILDLIKE FAITH

"Like as a father pitieth his children, so the Lord pitieth them that fear Him. For He knoweth our frame; He remembereth that we are dust"—Psalm ciii.13-14.

"THE life and work of Hudson Taylor were founded upon three facts, namely that 'There is a Living God; He has spoken in the Bible; and He means what He says, and will do all He has promised'. There was no title he more loved to use for God than 'FATHER'. And there was no attitude he more rejoiced to adopt than that of a trustful child.

'I do not believe,' he wrote, 'that our Heavenly Father will ever forget His children. I am a very poor father, but it is not my habit to forget my children. God is a very, very good Father. It is not His habit to forget His children.'

'It is not difficult for me to remember that my little ones need breakfast in the morning, dinner at mid-day, and something before they go to bed at night. Indeed, I could not forget it. And I find it impossible to suppose that our Heavenly Father is less tender or mindful than I.'

His belief in Psalm ciii. 13-14 was the secret of his strength and peace, and this calm trustfulness in God as his Father was one of the greatest legacies he left behind him. Hudson Taylor's simple, child-like faith, stood all the stern tests of an exacting life and heart-rending sorrows, and he still continued 'steadfast, unmoveable, always abounding in the work of the Lord.' He never could exhaust the infinite wealth of these simple words: 'Like a Father.' "

"Trusting as a little child,
Help us, Lord, to be
While we ask, in simple faith,
Deeper love to Thee."

ONLY BELIEVE !

To obtain deliverances.

" O Daniel, servant of the living God, is thy God, . . . able to deliver thee from the lions ? . . . Daniel was taken up out of the den, and no manner of hurt was found upon him, because he believed in his God."—Dan. vi. 20-23.

" DARIUS doubted God because he did not know Him. Daniel was living and triumphant because he knew the secret of the Most High and dwelt under His shadow (Psl. xci. 1). And the God of Daniel is as mighty to-day as He has been from all Eternity. It is those who know Him who do exploits. Faith is the sufficient reply to every advance of unbelief, whether it issue from atheistic headquarters of Communism, or the lecture desk of a so-called Christian university. . . .

The boastful challenge of the Adversary rings with increasing defiance, through the gathering darkness of these days—' Is thy God able ? ' With exultant faith the true servant of the Lord can lift up his head and answer, ' Our God, Whom we serve, is able . . . and He will.' Is it a matter of personal salvation ? ' He is able to save unto the uttermost.' Of weakness ? He is able to keep us ' from falling.' Of doubt ? ' He is able to succour them that are tempted.' Of final perseverance ? ' He is able to keep that which I have committed unto Him against that day.' Is it a matter of the promises ? What He has promised, He is able also to perform. Is it ability to serve or to give ? ' He is able to make all grace super-abound unto you, that ye always, having all-sufficiency in all things, may super-abound unto every good work.' Does it concern Israel in unbelief ? ' He is able to graft them in again ? ' Every interest of the child of God, from the personal and physical needs to the great problems of the outer world, can be safely and quietly left to that ' working ' whereby ' He is able even to subdue all things unto Himself.' "

—J.A.M., in " Christian Alliance Weekly."

**" 'Tis the grandest theme, let the tidings roll
To the burdened heart, to the sinful soul,
Look to God in faith, He will make you whole:
Our God is able to deliver thee.
He is able to deliver Thee ;
Tho' by care oppressed,
Go to Him for rest,—
Our God is able to deliver thee."**

TRUSTING AND RESTING

"He that cometh to God must believe that He is, and that He is a rewarder of them that diligently seek Him"—Heb. xi.6.

"I DO beg of you to recognise the extreme simplicity of faith, that it is nothing more or less than just believing God when He says He either has done something for us, or will do it; and then trusting Him to do it. It is so simple that it is hard to explain. If anyone asks me what it means to trust another to do a piece of work for me, I can only answer that it means letting that other one do it, and feeling it perfectly unnecessary for me to do it myself. Every one of us has trusted very important pieces of work to others in this way, and has felt perfect rest in thus trusting, because of the confidence we have had in those who have undertaken to do it. . . . Trusting, therefore, simply means that when we have yielded ourselves up to the Lord, or, in other words, have made ourselves over to Him, we then have perfect confidence that He will manage us, and everything concerning us, exactly right, and we consequently leave the whole care and managing in His hands. There is nothing but common-sense in this. It is what we do a hundred times a day with our fellow-men. . . . And, if we find it an easy and natural thing to do this toward man, how much more easy it must be to do it toward God."

Hannah Whitall Smith.

"It is strange we trust each other,
And only doubt our Lord;
We will take the word of mortals,
And yet distrust His Word;
But, oh, what light and glory
Would shine o'er all our days,
If we always would remember
That He means just what He says."

(*Rev. A. B. Simpson, D.D.*)

ONLY BELIEVE !

To avert Satanic "blinding."

"The god of this world hath blinded the minds of them which believe not, lest the light of the glorious Gospel of Christ, who is the image of God, should shine unto them." —II Cor. iv. 4.

"IT takes more faith to believe that the Bible is a merely human book than it does to believe that it is the Word of God. The things of God are spiritually discerned, but the agnostic is spiritually blind. Therefore he says, 'the Bible is false.' The sceptic reads the Bible, but he is not moved to worship. He says that it is a book of contradictions, of absurdities, and idle fables. The man of intellectual pride reads it without being warmed, for he merely compiles from it statistics of evidences, authorships, and dates. The man of worldly wisdom condescends to read it, but comes away not with reverent amazement, but with schemes for moral or worldly improvement, throwing away much of the book as puerile, sentimentality, or obsolete superstition. Anybody who has learned to spell can read the book, but only those who have received their sight, at the hands of the Author, can behold the wonders that lie hidden beneath the veil of the text.

Believers need not apologize for their *faith*. Do not let the things that you do not know, interfere with the things that you do know. Do not let the agnostic pity us for our faith. If he discredits the Bible, remember that thousands of years of history only tend to establish it, and the burden of proof lies, not on some embarrassed Christian, but on the scoffer himself. It is he who, glorying in his uncertainty, has nothing on which to lean. Let him who harps on the idea that he is in the dark, and 'not sure of anything,' read those words thoughtfully :—'I am come a light into the world, that *whosoever believeth* on Me should not abide in darkness' (John xii. 46). 'I am the light of the world ; he that followeth Me shall not walk in darkness but shall have the light of life' (John viii. 12)."

—Victor Arundel, in "Moody Monthly."

"Within this sacred volume lies
The mystery of mysteries !
Happiest they of human race,
To whom their God has granted grace
To read, to fear, to hope, to pray,
To lift the latch, and force the way;
And better they had ne'er been born,
Who read to doubt, or read to scorn."

(*Sir Walter Scott.*)

COMMITTING OUR WAY

"Commit thy way unto the Lord; *trust also* in Him; and He shall bring it to pass"—Psalm xxxvii.5.

" 'COMMIT thy way unto the Lord *and trust*!'
Oh! it is here we fail. We give the wheel
Of our small barque to Him; but then we thrust
Our hand upon His hand,
And dare to stand
Beside our Master, lest He wreck our keel.

'Commit thy way unto the Lord *and trust*!'
Leave all to Him: believe He knows thy course,
Thy dangers, and thy safety—all—then just
Abandon all to Him:
So shalt thou skim
Borne briskly on before the Spirit's force.

'Commit thy way unto the Lord *and trust*!'
There is an 'also' we too oft forget—
And so are plagued and worried. Oh! we must
'Trust also'—then our sail
Shall cease to roll
In restlessness and reason and regret.

Commit! and when committed, trust His Word!
Has He not said that He will bring thee through?
Trust His strong arm; and when wild storms are heard,
Believe He holds them still
By His strong will,
Trust Him, the Wise, the Faithful, and the True.

Trust Him to manage all that thou dost now
Commit to Him—the ship, the sails, the sea,
The sailors—thy strange crew. And ask not how
He will do all for thee,
But trustful be.
Lie down and rest, from anxious worry free."

(*William Luff.*)

ONLY BELIEVE!

To receive the filling of the Spirit.

" Be filled with the Spirit."—Eph. v. 18.

"TWO words are, I believe, the secret of the infilling of the Holy Spirit—Obedience and Faith. Are you prepared to obey God? That may sound quite simple. It is easy to say 'Yes.' Are you prepared to obey Him in whatever command He lays upon you? Are you prepared, business man, to obey God in your business? It may very seriously affect your business. Are you prepared to obey God in your home? There might be very serious readjustments of relationships if you are going to obey God in your home. Are you prepared to obey God in what you call your Christian service? You have your programme, have you not? Are you prepared for that programme to be scrapped, because it centres round you?

Well, if you are prepared to do that, that is the first step. The second step is faith. What is faith? You do not need any fresh definition. Faith is receiving. Obedience and receiving. Are you prepared, at this moment, to receive this fullness of God's Holy Spirit, apart altogether from any emotion, apart altogether from any ecstatic feeling? Are you prepared, just by *a simple act of faith*, to receive the fullness of God's Holy Spirit? It will mean all the difference in the coming days: instead of powerless service, there will be service of power; instead of cowardice there will be courage; instead of a dull mind there is going to be an understanding of, and a love for God's Word. A great many other differences are going to happen if you are willing, even now, in obedience and simple faith, to receive God's infilling of His Holy Spirit. . . . There will be many subsequent 'fillings'—that was true of the early disciples—but there will be the first filling. Will that be now?"

—*Rev. W. H. Aldis.*

" I take the promised Holy Ghost,
I take the power of Pentecost,
To fill me to the uttermost,
'I take'—'He undertakes.'"

(***Rev. A. B. Simpson.***)

THE WAY OF ESCAPE

"Thy Father!" "Your heavenly Father knoweth"—Matt. vi.4,32.

"TO make all things quiet in the soul, even for a moment to concentrate on an attribute of God and let the wonder of it fill the heart, that is the way of escape from the exasperations and the trivialities of life.

On the last night of his life, Dr. Chalmers, sauntering in his garden, was overheard earnestly repeating, 'Father, my Father!' The General Assembly was in progress, and the burden and responsibilities of the Church were heavy upon him. But there, in the stillness of meditation, he came to God in a way which is open to the simplest."

Rev. W. M. Macgregor, D.D.

"There is something about deep sorrow that tends to wake up the *child*-feeling in all of us. A man of great intellect becomes like a little child when a great grief smites him, or when a grave opens beneath his bedroom or his fireside. . . . So, a Christian, in the time of trouble, is brought to his child-feeling. He wants to lean somewhere, to talk to somebody, to have somebody love him and hold him up. His extremity becomes God's opportunity. Then his humbled spirit cries out—

"O Lord! a little, helpless child
Comes to Thee this day for rest;
Take me, fold me in Thy arms,
Hold my head upon Thy breast.'

One great purpose in all affliction is to bring us down to the everlasting arms. . . . Faith, in its essence, is simply a resting on the everlasting arms. It is trusting them and not our weakness. Faith is just the clinging to those arms and nothing more."

Rev. Theodore L. Cuyler, D.D.

ONLY BELIEVE !

To make our Walk acceptable.

" We walk by faith, not by sight."—II Cor. v. 7.

"ALL God's children are called to walk by faith, and faith is needed to deal aright with property or business, or to fill any position in a manner worthy of Christ. We can only carry out the Lord's exhortation, 'Seek ye first the kingdom of God and His righteousness,' as we truly receive the promise that follows, 'and all these things (which, He had just said, your heavenly Father knoweth that ye have need of) shall be added unto you.' Of Robert Chapman, of Barnstaple, it was said, 'One great object—it may be said *the* great object—of his ministry, public and private, was *to encourage and strengthen faith*, and to show the folly, as well as the sin, of unbelief. He was told of a sister in Scotland who had once been in 'easier circumstances,' but having used her all in the service of Christ, said she had now nothing to look to *but* 'the Living God.' Mr. Chapman calmly replied, 'Tell that sister, from me, that I would not give up that 'BUT' for all the gold in the Bank of England.'

Take out of life the bitterness of unbelieving fears, the bitterness of mortified pride, and the bitterness of self-will, and there will be very little left that is not sweet.

If we walk in true fellowship with the Father and the Son, by the Spirit, and recognise that all our matters are ordered by our Heavenly Father in perfect wisdom and love, we must be giving thanks; but if we treat our matters simply as *our own*, seek to deal with them by our own wisdom, have regard to their results only as they concern ourselves, and fail to bring God into them all, in the spirit of faith, with the assurance that He controls them for His own glory and our truest blessing, our harp will soon be hung on the willows."—*W. H. Bennet.*

" Keep up the song of faith,
However dark the night ;
And, as you praise, the Lord will work
To change your faith to sight."
(M. E. Barber).

BETTER THAN SPARROWS

"Behold the fowls of the air: for they sow not, neither do they reap, nor gather into barns; yet your heavenly Father feedeth them. Are ye not much better than they?"—Matt. vi.26.

"Fear ye not therefore, ye are of more value than many sparrows"—Matt. x.31.

"HERE is a sermon against fear, and *sparrows* are the text. . . . The birds are fed by God; will He not feed us? They are free from the fret which comes of hoarding and trading; why should not we be? If God feeds the fowls of the air without sowing, or reaping, or storing, surely He will supply us when we trustfully use these means. For us to rely upon these means, and forget our God, would be folly indeed. . . . Oh, that we would be as good as the birds in trustfulness, since, in dignity of nature, we are 'so much better than they.' "

Rev. C. H. Spurgeon.

"I am only a little sparrow!
A bird of low degree:
My life is of little value,
But the dear Lord cares for me.

. . . . . .

I have no barn or storehouse,
I neither sow nor reap;
God gives me a sparrow's portion,
But never a seed to keep.

If my meat is sometimes scanty,
Close picking makes it sweet;
I have always enough to feed me,
And 'Life is more than meat.'

I know there are many sparrows—
All over the world they're found;
But our Heavenly Father knoweth
When one of us falls to the ground.

Though small, we are never forgotten,
Though weak, we are never afraid;
For we know that the dear Lord keepeth
The lives of the creatures He made."

(*Anon.*)

ONLY BELIEVE !

To avoid dishonouring God.

" O thou of little faith, wherefore didst thou doubt ? "— Matt. xiv. 31.

" IS it possible that you can trust your fellow-men and cannot trust your God ? That you can receive the 'witness of men,' and cannot receive the 'witness of God' ? That you can believe man's records, and cannot believe God's record ? That you can commit your dearest earthly interests to your weak, failing fellow-creatures without a fear, and are afraid to commit your spiritual interests to the blessed Saviour Who shed His blood for the very purpose of saving you, and who is declared to be 'able to save you to the uttermost' ?

Surely, surely, dear believer, you whose very name of '*believer*' implies that you can believe, you will never again excuse yourself on the plea of having no faith. For, when you say this, you mean, of course, that you have no faith in God ; for you are not asked to have faith in yourself, and you would be in a very wrong condition of soul if you had. Let me beg of you, then, when you think or say these things, always to complete the sentence, and say, 'I have no faith in God, I cannot believe God' ; and this, I am sure, will soon become so dreadful to you, that you will not dare to continue it.

Put your will, then, over on to the believing side. Say, 'Lord, I will believe, I do believe,' and continue to say it. Insist upon believing, in the face of every suggestion of doubt which Satan may bring. Out of your very unbelief, throw yourself headlong on to the promises of God, and dare to abandon yourself to the keeping and saving power of the Lord Jesus. If you have ever trusted a precious interest in the hands of any earthly friend, I conjure you, trust yourself now, and all your spiritual interest, in the hands of your Heavenly Friend, and never, never, NEVER, allow yourself to doubt again."

—*H.W.S., in " The Christian's Secret of a Happy Life."*

" All things are possible to him
  That can in Jesus' name believe ;
Lord, I no more Thy name blaspheme,
  Thy truth I lovingly receive.
I can, I do believe in Thee ;
All things are possible to me."

(*Charles Wesley.*)

THE WORD OF A GENTLEMAN

"Lo, I am with you alway, even unto the end of the age"—Matt. xxviii.20.

"Now the God of hope fill you with all joy and peace in believing"—Rom. xv.13.

"JANUARY 14th, 1856. Evening. Felt much turmoil of spirit in prospect of having all my plans for the welfare of this great region, and this teeming population, knocked on the head by savages to-morrow. But I read that Jesus said: 'All power is given unto Me in heaven and in earth. Go ye therefore, and teach all nations, and lo, I am with you alway, even unto the end of the age.' It is the word of a gentleman of the most strict and sacred honour, so there's an end of it! I will not cross furtively to-night as I intended. Should such a man as I flee? Nay, verily, I shall take observations for latitude and longitude to-night, though they may be the last. *I feel quite calm now, thank God*!"

Extract from "Dr. Livingstone's Journal".

"Calm me, my God, and keep me calm,
While these hot breezes blow;
Be like the night-dew's cooling balm
Upon earth's fevered brow.

Calm me, my God, and keep me calm
Soft resting on Thy breast;
Soothe me with holy hymn and psalm,
And bid my spirit rest.

Yes, keep me calm, though loud and rude
The sounds my ear that greet:
Calm in the closet's solitude,
Calm in the bustling street.

Calm in the hour of buoyant health,
Calm in my hour of pain,
Calm in my poverty or wealth,
Calm in my loss or gain.

Calm 'mid the restless heaving throng,
Who do not know Thy name;
Calm in the sufferance of wrong,
Like Him who bore my shame.

Calm as the ray of sun or star
Which storms assail in vain;
Moving unruffled through earth's war,
The eternal calm to gain." (*Dr. Horatius Bonar.*)

ONLY BELIEVE !

To manifest loyal confidence in Jesus.

" Your lives should be untainted by love for money. Be content with what you have ; for God Himself has said, ' I will never, never let go your hand ; I will never, never forsake you ' (Gen. xxviii. 15, Deut. xxxi. 6-8, Josh. 1. 5). So that we fearlessly say, ' The Lord is my Helper ; I will not be afraid : what can man do to me ' (Psl. cxviii. 6)." —Heb. xiii. 5, 6 (Weymouth).

" ' YOU have not passed this way heretofore,' it may be ; but to-day it is your happy privilege to prove, as never before, your loyal confidence in Jesus by starting out with Him on a life and walk of faith, lived moment by moment in absolute and child-like trust in Him. You have trusted Him in a few things, and He has not failed you. Trust Him now for everything ; and see if He does not do for you exceeding abundantly above all that you could ever have asked or thought, not according to your power or capacity, but according to His own mighty power, that will work in you all the good pleasure of His most blessed will.

You find no difficulty in trusting the Lord with the management of the universe, and all the outward creation, and can your case be any more complex or difficult than these, that you need to be anxious or troubled about the management of it ? Away with such unworthy doubtings ! Take your stand on the power and trustworthiness of your God, and see how quickly all difficulties will vanish for a *steadfast determination to believe*. Trust in the dark, trust in the light, trust at night, and trust in the morning, and you will find that the faith, which may begin with a mighty effort, will end sooner or later by becoming the easy and natural habit of the soul."

—*H.W.S., in " The Christian's Secret of a Happy Life."*

" Standing on the promises that cannot fail,
When the howling storms of doubt and fear assail,
By the living Word of God I shall prevail,—
Standing on the promises of God."

(*R.K.C.*)

TRUSTING OMNIPOTENCE

"He careth for *you*"—I Peter v.7.
"Let not your heart be troubled"—John xiv.1.
"Be not afraid, only believe"—Mark v.36.

" 'HE shall feed His flock like a shepherd!' Who is this? Is it that God whose throne is immutability—whose power is boundless—whose dominion is immensity—whose life-time is eternity. Yet He, with a shepherd's love and tenderness, attends to the wants of the humblest and weakest of His enormous family;—feeding all His flock, and marking the peculiarities of all. There is no subject of contemplation, indeed, more marvellous, than the unceasing attention and care lavished by Deity on *small* as well as *great*; that the vast provinces of His great empire do not withdraw His thoughts and care from the feeble and insignificant; that He who wheels the planets in their courses, and lights up the blazing suns of the firmament, can watch also the sparrows fall, and feed the young ravens when they cry! Just as the mountain supports the tiny blade of grass and the modest floweret, as well as the giant pine or cedar; just as the ocean bears up in safety the sea-bird seated on its crested waves, as well as the leviathan vessel; so while the Great Keeper of Israel can listen to the archangel's song, and the seraph's burning devotions, He can carry in His bosom the feeblest lamb of the fold, and lead gently the most sorrowing spirit."

Rev. J. R. Macduff, D.D.

"Among so many, can HE care?
Can special love be everywhere—
A myriad homes—a myriad ways,
And God's eye over every place?
I asked. My soul bethought of this—
In just that very place of HIS
Where He hath put, and keepeth you,
God hath no other thing to do."

(*Anon.*)

ONLY BELIEVE !

To discover God's faithfulness.

" The word of the Lord came unto Abram, saying, Fear not, Abram ; I am thy shield, and thy exceeding great reward. . . . And *he believed the Lord* ; and He counted it to him for righteousness."—Gen. xv. 1-6.

" 'AND Abram BELIEVED '! This is the first time the word ' believed ' occurs in the Bible. . . . Believed,—what a history opens in this one word ! The moment Abram believed he was truly born again. We may see here some of the great meanings of the word. Paul says of Abram that, ' against hope he believed in hope,' and ' that he staggered not at the promise of God through unbelief.' Here, then, we may study the word at the fountain head. ' Believed ' means *supported, sustained, strengthened* ; Abram nourished and nurtured himself in God ; Abram hid his life and his future in this promise as a child might hide or nestle in a mother's breast. *That* is faith. He took the promise as a fulfilment ; the word was to him a *fact*. Thus he was called out of himself, out of his own trust, out of his own resources, and his life was fostered upon God,—he by-lived, lived by, believed God ! It was surely a perilous moment. Appearances were against the promise. Doubt might well have said, ' How can this thing be ? ' But Abram ' staggered not.' God's love was set before him like an open door, and Abram went in and became a child at home. . . . To believe, is not simply to assent ; it is to take the thing *promised* as if it were actually *given*. . . . What Abram did we ourselves have to do. He rested on the word of God ; he did not wait until the child was born, and then say ' *Now* I believe.' *That* would not have been *faith*, it would have been *sight*. It is thus that I must believe God : I must throw my whole soul upon Him, and drive all doubt, all fear, from my heart, and take the promise as a fact. God asks me to do so ; He says He will give me strength to do so. . . . See how large a life Abram entered into when he believed ! He became a contemporary of all ages ; a citizen and freeman of all cities the world over and time without end."—*Dr. Joseph Parker.*

'Lord. give me such a faith as this,
And then, whate'er may come,
I'll taste e'en now the hallowed bliss
Of an eternal home."

WHEN I'M AFRAID

"I will trust, and not be afraid"—Isa. xii.2.

"What time I am afraid I will trust in Thee"—Psalm lvi.3.

"WHEN I'm afraid of times before,
  What coming days will bring;
When life's omissions I deplore,
  And earth-mists round me cling.
O Lord of love, my weakness see;
  When I'm afraid I'll trust in Thee.

When I'm afraid of wily foes,
  Their flattery and hate—
Who seek my progress to oppose,
  My joys to dissipate:
O Lord of hosts, my weakness see;
  When I'm afraid I'll trust in Thee.

When I'm afraid of dangers near,
  Forboding future ills;
When rocks, and shoals, and deeps I fear,
  And gloom my spirit fills:
O Lord of might, my weakness see;
  When I'm afraid I'll trust in Thee.

When I'm afraid of crushing loss,
  Parting from loved ones dear—
Lest I shall murmur at my cross,
  And yield to faithless fear;
O Lord of peace, my weakness see;
  When I'm afraid I'll trust in Thee.

When I'm afraid of failing health,
  Sore weaknesses I know—
And illness steals o'er me by stealth,
  And sickness lays me low;
O Lord of power, my weakness see;
  When I'm afraid I'll trust in Thee.

When I'm afraid of drear old age,
  As nature's powers decay;
Mortality's dread heritage,
  Increasing day by day;
O Lord of grace, my weakness see;
  When I'm afraid I'll trust in Thee."

(*A. Gardner.*)

ONLY BELIEVE !

To abound in hope.

" Now the God of hope fill you with all joy and peace in believing, that ye may abound in hope."—Rom. xv. 13.

"DID you ever notice this—that no man or woman who has lost hope is ever used by God to build up His kingdom? . . . A man filled with the Spirit of God will be very hopeful : he will be looking out into the future, and he knows that it is all bright, because the God of all grace is able to do great things. So, it is very important that we have hope.

Some years ago, I was quite discouraged in my work, and was ready to hang my harp upon the willow. I was very much cast down and depressed. I had been for weeks in that state, when one Monday morning a friend, who had a very large Bible-class, came into my study. I used to examine the notes of his Sunday-school lessons, which were equal to a sermon, and he came to me this morning and said, 'Well, what did you preach about yesterday?' and I told him. I said, 'What did you preach about?' And he said that he preached about Noah. 'Did you ever preach about Noah?' said he. 'No, I never preached about Noah.' 'Did you ever study his character?' 'No, I never studied his life particularly.' 'Well,' says he, 'he is a most wonderful character. It will do you good to consider it. You ought to study that character.' When he went out, I took down my Bible and read about Noah; and then it came over me that Noah worked a hundred and twenty years and never made a convert; and yet he did not get discouraged. Then said I, 'Well, I ought not to be discouraged,' and I closed my Bible, got up, and walked down town; and the cloud had gone. I went down to the noon prayer-meeting, and heard of a little town in the country where they had taken into church a hundred young converts: and I said to myself, 'I wonder what Noah would have given if he could have heard that'; and yet he worked a hundred and twenty years and did not get discouraged. . . . . O, children of God, let us not get discouraged; let us ask God to forgive us, if we have been discouraged and cast down; let us ask God to give us 'hope,' that we may be ever hopeful."—*D. L. Moody*.

" Do you ever feel down-hearted or discouraged?
Do you ever think your work is all in vain?
Do the burdens thrust upon you make you tremble,
And you fear that you shall ne'er the victory gain

Have faith in God,—the sun will shine,—
Though dark the clouds may be to-day;
His heart hath planned your path and mine
Have faith in God, have faith alway."

TAKING GOD AT HIS WORD

"I trust in Thy Word"—Psalm cxix.42.

"Great peace have they which love Thy law: and nothing shall offend (stumble) them"—Psalm cxix.165.

"A MAN once said to me, 'What do you do with what you don't understand?' 'I don't do anything with it.' 'How do you understand it?' 'I don't understand it.' 'Well, how do you interpret it?' 'I don't interpret it.' 'What do you do with it?' 'I don't do anything with it.' 'Don't do anything with it? Do you believe it?' 'Yes, I believe it.' Of course I do. I am glad there is a height I know nothing about in the old Book, a length and a breadth we know nothing about. It makes the Book all the more fascinating. I thank God it is beyond me. It is a pretty good proof that it came from God and not from the hand of man. You can take a chapter and read it for 365 days in the year, and always find something new in that chapter. Read this Book; study it and do what it tells you, and you will grow to love it." *D. L. Moody.*

"Faith is not a sense, nor sight, nor reason, but taking God at His word." *Evans.*

"The same old baffling questions! O, my friend,
I cannot answer them. In vain I send
My soul into the dark, where never burn
The lamps of Science, nor the natural light
Of Reason's sun and stars! . . .

. . . . .

I have no answer for myself or thee,
Save that I learned beside my mother's knee;
'All is of God that is, and is to be;
And God is good.' Let this suffice us still,
Resting in *child-like trust* upon His will
Who moves to His great ends, unthwarted by the ill."
(*Whittier.*)

ONLY BELIEVE !

To know the triumph of Faith.

" Take now thy son, . . . and get thee into the land of Moriah ; and offer him there for a burnt offering."— Gen. xxii. 2.

" THE experience of Abraham and our own experience are strikingly coincident, in the fact that we are often exposed to great trials *without any reason being assigned for their infliction.* Notice this in the case of Abraham. In the very midst of his domestic joy this desolating word falls. We do not read that Abraham had been committing sin, or that in any way he had been provoking the Most High to anger. From one point of view this trial is wholly without cause or reason, and the terms read like an edict of wanton and ruthless cruelty.

Such experiences are far from uncommon in our own day. We see human fortunes reversed without any apparent reason ; the innocent are impoverished and scourged ; men are paralysed in the very attitude and act of prayer ; honestly gotten wealth is scattered beyond recovery ; the most useful workers in the Church are laid aside by sickness ; and they who would gladly be foremost in the fight, are made to stand still because of pain and helplessness. No reason is given. No justification is offered. The fearful demand is made point-blank, and no compromise is possible. God sometimes insists upon a distinct ' Yes ' or ' No,' and then to falter is to rebel.

When such trials are accepted in a filial spirit, the triumph of faith is complete. Such faith is counted unto men for righteousness. It is not a faith that hesitates and falters and struggles ; it is a faith victorious ; in its way, even infinite and omnipotent. . . .

We are not called upon to give up one taste out of many ; one wish out of many ; we are distinctly called upon to give up everything—to sink our will in God's ; to be no longer our own ; to sum up every prayer with, ' Nevertheless, not my will but Thine be done.' That is pure religion before God and the Father. ' Except a man deny himself, and take up his cross daily, he *cannot* be My disciple.' "—*Dr. Joseph Parker.*

" If Thou shouldst call me to resign
What most I prize, it ne'er was mine
I only yield Thee what was Thine
Thy will be done ! "

REDEMPTION FOR SINNERS

"Come unto ME, all ye that labour and are heavy laden, and I will give you rest"—Matt. xi.28.

"Him that cometh to ME I will in no wise cast out"—John vi.37.

"SOULS of men! Why will ye scatter
  Like a crowd of frightened sheep?
Foolish hearts, why will ye wander
  From a love so true and deep?

Was there ever kindest shepherd
  Half so gentle, half so sweet,
As the Saviour, who would have us
  Come and gather round His feet?

There's a wideness in God's mercy,
  Like the wideness of the sea:
There's a kindness in His justice
  Which is more than liberty.

For the love of God is broader
  Than the measures of man's mind;
And the heart of the Eternal
  Is most wonderfully kind.

There is plentiful redemption
  In the blood that has been shed:
There is joy for all the members
  In the sorrows of the Head.

Pining souls! come nearer JESUS,
  And, O come, not doubting thus,
But *with faith that trusts more bravely*
  His great tenderness for us.

If our love were but more simple
  We should take Him at His word;
And our lives would be all sunshine
  In the sweetness of our Lord."

Faber.

ONLY BELIEVE !

To be safely led.

" I will bring the blind by a way that they knew not ; I will lead them in paths that they have not known : I will make darkness light before them, and crooked things straight. These things will I do unto them and not forsake them."—Isa. xlii. 16.

" He leadeth me."—Psl. xxiii. 2.

" WHAT a wondrous link between these two personal pronouns, ' He leadeth me ' ! As in the East, the shepherd always precedes the flock, to discover the greenest patches of grass and the least stony path, so does Jesus ever keep in front of the soul that ever trusts and loves Him. We must be willing to be led. There is so much natural impetuosity in us to shoot on in front and ' prospect ' for ourselves. Is that not so ?

And, out of this restlessness, there arises so much of the fret and chafe and disappointment of life. We think we can do so much better for ourselves than Christ can do for us. We doubt whether there is not something outside the limit of His will, which it might be worth our while to snatch at. We are inclined to run before or linger behind, or go off to forage on the right or left. We take a long time ere we learn that the place of usefulness and blessedness is in following the lead of Jesus. The one ambition of our being should be to be sure that we are resolutely following the Shepherd whithersoever He goeth. According to His own assurance, when He putteth forth His own sheep, He goeth before them, and the sheep follow Him."—*Dr. F. B. Meyer.*

" He leadeth me ! Oh, blessed thought !
Oh words with heavenly comfort fraught !
Whate'er I do, where'er I be,
Still 'tis God's hand that leadeth me.

Sometimes 'mid scenes of deepest gloom,
Sometimes where Eden's bowers bloom,
By waters calm, o'er troubled sea—
Still 'tis God's hand that leadeth me."

FEAR VERSUS TRUST

"Fear not: only believe" (trust)—Luke viii.50 (R.V.)

"THOSE words, spoken by Christ to Jairus, have been a golden counsel to millions of inquiring souls, and a golden comfort to millions of afflicted saints. Fear not; only trust! The one brings torment; the other brings peace. Doubt always disquiets. Trust calms the troubled heart, as Christ's omnipotent voice calmed Galilee's tempest into smooth unruffled stillness. Doubt cripples all exertion. A doubting inquirer is not ready to pray as he ought, or to obey as he ought. Faith prompts to pray for help, and then to do what Jesus bids. Doubt dishonours Christ; insults Him. Trust takes Him at His word, and believes that He can save a soul already dead in trespasses and sin. 'I found I had nothing *to do but trust* Him,' said an intelligent convert to her pastor, after many weeks of distress had ended in serene peace. And these words, 'Fear not; only trust!' were the manna which we gave to a dying friend last week. He said that they prepared him to feel 'safe in the arms of Jesus'.

Kind reader, you and I have some hard climbing to do before we reach the top. We must imitate Alpine climbers, and keep strong hold of the Guide. Let us take short views. If we look over the precipices, we shall grow dizzy. If we look *too* far ahead, we shall grow discouraged. Let us rather put our weak hands into Christ's strong, loving grasp, and all the time listen to His cheering words, 'Fear not; only TRUST!' "

Theodore L. Cuyler, D.D.

ONLY BELIEVE !

To triumph in adversity.

" By faith ye stand."—II Cor. i. 24.

"FAITH refuses to despair even on the blackest night : rejoices in Christ Jesus however contrary the winds ; and rides out the fiercest storm because anchored in the Rock.

Faith trusts and obeys in the dark. However far away the Eternal Friend may seem (judging by present events), faith's unwavering language is : ' Thou *art* near, O Lord.'

Faith lives in certainties, and, believing the promises, acts on them, no matter how apparently adverse earthly circumstances may be.

Faith never loses sight of the Crowned Christ who has overcome the world : and so faith quietly rests in the Lord and waits patiently for Him.

Faith overcomes because Faith sees the Victorious Saviour through everything. Thus faith's outlook is always bright. . . . God has His own wise purpose, and His own ways. Strange, indeed, they are to the flesh, but faith recognizes ' it is the Lord,' and submits to His hand, knowing that He works within to will and to do of His good pleasure. Nothing but gain can come through trusting the Lord."—*H. Arthur Woolley.*

" Precious thought, my Father knoweth,
In His love I rest ;
For whate'er my Father doeth
Must be always best :
Well I know the heart that planneth
Nought but good for me,—
Joy and Sorrow interwoven—
Love in all I see.

Oh, to trust Him then more fully !
Just to simply move
In the conscious, calm enjoyment
Of the Father's love ;
Knowing that life's chequered pathway
Leadeth to His rest ;
Satisfied the way He taketh
Must be always best."

THE CRY OF THE SINNER

"He endured, as seeing HIM who is invisible"—Heb. xi.27.

"Jesus Christ, whom having not seen, ye love: in whom, though now ye see Him not, yet *believing*, ye rejoice with joy unspeakable and full of glory: receiving the end of your faith, even the salvation of your souls"—I Peter i.8-9.

"Blessed are they that have not seen, and yet *have believed.*" —John xx.29.

"I TRUST the *Cross* of Jesus! 'twas for me
He bore that cross—it was my cross He bore,
My sin, my curse, that I, from sin set free,
Might sing His praise, and His free love adore.

I trust the *life* of Jesus! 'twas for me
He lived, and toiled, and did the Father's will:
That in His life God's holy eye might see
A perfect life, that should His law fulfil.

I trust the *heart* of Jesus! 'twas for me
That heart poured forth its love in streams of life,
That I might wash, that I refreshed might be,
And find a fountain 'mid earth's desert strife.

I trust the *hand* of Jesus! pierced for me,
The hand held fast by nails now holds me fast.
And if I sink, as, walking life's rough sea,
This rescues me, and stills the raging blast.

I trust the loving Jesus! Christ for me!
For me in death, for me upon His throne:
His name, His blood, His righteousness my plea:
He is my hope, my life, and He alone.

And does some trembler say, "'Tis thus I trust'?
Then thou art saved. His death atones for thee;
Thy punishment is past: thy pardon just:
Rejoice and sing, 'The Saviour died for me!' "

William Luff.

ONLY BELIEVE !

To obtain answers to prayer.

" This is the confidence that we have in Him, that, if we ask anything according to His will, He heareth us."— I John v. 14.

"OUR universal remedy for all our difficulties is—Prayer, Faith, and Patience. The philosophy of holy living. The beginning of anxiety is the end of faith ; and the beginning of true faith is the end of all anxiety.

Faith is developed—or increased—by clinging to the Word of God, looking for its fulfilment in the time of need, expecting the answer to prayers, and to do this in spite of all contrary appearances. As I began 65 years and 8 months since, so I continue, and am not in the least tired of this life of entire dependence on God ; nay, the very reverse, it is a delightful task to me, to roll all my burdens upon God, and to speak to Him about everything, as anyone would open his heart to his bosom friend.

I wish to direct the Church of God at large to the fact that God is what He was in the days of the prophets and apostles, ever willing and able to answer the prayers of His children, when they ask for things according to His mind (I John v. 14) : if they ask on the ground of the merits and worthiness of the Lord Jesus ; *viz.*, in His Name (John xiv. 14) : if they *believe* that God is able and willing to answer their prayer (Mark xi. 24) : if they do not live in sin (Psl. lxvi. 18), and if they go on in *believing prayer*, till the answer is given ; for God has not fixed a time, when our prayer shall be answered."—*George Müller.*

" Unanswered yet ? The pray'r your lips have pleaded
In agony of heart these many years ?
Does faith begin to fail ? Is hope departing ?
And think you all in vain those falling tears ?
Say not the Father hath not heard your prayer,
You shall have your desire, sometime, somewhere.

Unanswered yet ? Nay, do not say ' ungranted ' ;
Perhaps your part is not yet wholly done ;
The work began when first your prayer was uttered,
And God will finish what He has begun ;
If you will keep the incense burning there,
His glory you shall see sometime, somewhere."

UNFAILING FAITHFULNESS

"Who is among you that feareth the Lord, that obeyeth the voice of His servant, that walketh in darkness, and hath no light? Let him *trust* in the name of the Lord, and stay upon his God"—Isa. 1.10.

"I will bring the blind by a way that they knew not; I will lead them in paths that they have not known: I will make darkness light before them, and crooked things straight. These things will I do unto them, and not forsake them"—Isa. xlii.16.

"Thou wilt keep him in perfect peace, whose mind is stayed on Thee: because he trusteth in Thee"—Isa. xxvi.3.

"WHEN the believer cannot close with a promise, he may lay hold on an attribute and say: 'Though my heart and flesh fail, God's faithfulness cannot; though I can scarcely discern sun, moon, or stars, yet will I cast anchor in the dark; I shall ride it out in safety till the shadows are fled.' "

"When darkness seems to veil His face,
I rest on His unchanging grace."

"The clouds hang heavy around my way:
I cannot see.
But through the darkness I believe
God leadeth me.

'Tis sweet to keep my hand in His
While all is dim;
To close my weary, aching eyes,
And follow Him.

Through many a stormy path He leads
My tiréd feet:
Through many a path of tears I go,
But it is sweet.

To know that He is close to me,
My God, my Guide!
He leadeth me, and so I walk
Quite satisfied.

To my blind eyes He may reveal
No light at all;
But while I lean on His strong arm
I cannot fall."

(*Anon.*)

ONLY BELIEVE !

To possess joy in sorrows.

" Lord, increase our faith."—Luke xvii. 5.

"IT were well if more Christians insisted on finding the ground of their faith, the reason why they are Christians. Their faith would then be stronger, and less easily shaken. When trouble comes, or any testing, it would continue firm and unmoved, because it rests on the rock of divine truth. . . . Doubt is always costly. It shuts out heavenly comfort. There are many Christian people who, especially in the first shock of sorrow, have an experience similar to that of Thomas. They shut themselves up with their grief, and refuse to accept the comfort of the Gospel of Christ. They turn away their ears from the voices of love which speak to them out of the Bible, and will not receive the divine consolations. The light shines all about them ; but they close doors and windows, and keep it from entering the darkened chamber where they sit. The music of peace floats on the air in sweet entrancing strains, but no gentle note finds its way to their hearts.

Too many Christian mourners fail to find comfort in sorrow. They believe the great truths of Christianity, that Jesus died for them and rose again ; but their faith fails them for the time in the hour of sorest distress. Meanwhile, they walk in darkness, as Thomas did. On the other hand, those who accept, and let into their hearts the great truths of Christ's resurrection, and the immortal life in Christ, feel the pain of parting no less sorely, but they find abundant consolation in the hope of eternal life for those whom they have lost for a time. . . . Faith is far better than doubt, confidence better than questioning. It is better to be a sunny Christian, rejoicing, songful, happy, than a sad, gloomy, despondent Christian. It makes one's own life sweeter and more beautiful. Then it makes others happier. A gloomy Christian casts dark shadows wherever he goes ; a sunny Christian is a benediction to every life he touches."—*Rev. J. R. Miller, D.D.*

**" Trusting in Jesus, oh, what should I fear ?
Nothing can harm me when He is so near
Sweet is the promise He giveth to me :
Oh, I am happy as mortal can be."**

A STEDFAST TRUST

"He giveth His beloved sleep"—Psalm cxxvii.2.

IT is related that on one occasion, when Dr. F. B. Meyer was visiting at the home of the Rev. E. Palgrave Davy, after lunch, he said he must just have twenty minutes' sleep before going to a meeting. "I was travelling much of the night, coming from the north, and I need a little rest." "All right," said his friend, "you go and lie down and I will come in and waken you in half-an-hour." "Oh, no!" he replied. "You mustn't do that. The Lord always wakes me up just when I ask Him. I say to Him, 'Lord, Thou knowest Thy child is tired and needs rest, and I have a meeting to address. Please give me a little sleep and wake me in twenty minutes;' and He always does, whatever time I ask Him. Oh, no; I mustn't let you waken me. That would seem as though I didn't trust Him." And, sure enough, he appeared in less than half-an-hour.

HIS CARE

"A tiny nest: three fledglings bare—
Three little mouths to feed:
A feathered mother's faithful care
To bring them all they need!

A dainty, snow-white covered bed—
Three little forms at rest;
A fair, a brown, a golden head,
And cheeks with crimson drest!

How sleep they thus without a care,
When nears the close of day?
A mother's heart and hands doth bear
Such burdens all away!

. . . . . .

And me—! may I find such repose,
When needs and cares assail?
My heart hath this—'My Father knows,
And HE CAN NEVER FAIL'."

(J. Danson Smith.)

ONLY BELIEVE !

To see the impossible accomplished.

"He staggered not at the promise of God through unbelief."—Rom. iv. 20.

"IT was a marvellous promise, that this childless pair should have a child, and become progenitors of a great nation, so that the stars of the heavenly vault, and the sand-grains on the ocean-shore, should not be more numerous. And it was enough to stagger any man to be told of it. But Abraham staggered not. How was this?

It did not arise from ignoring the difficulties that obstructed its realization—He might have done so. Whenever the natural obstacles arose in his mind, he might have ignored them. But this, according to the R.V. rendering of the previous verse, was not Abraham's policy. He quietly and deliberately considered the enormous difficulties that lay in the path of the Divine purpose, and in spite of them 'he staggered not.'

But his unstaggering faith arose from his great thoughts of Him Who had promised. He kept saying to himself, 'He is able; He is able.' He knew that God would not have said what He could not perform. He knew that the God of nature was Lord of the nature He had made. He knew that no word of the Almighty could be destitute of power. He fed his faith by cherishing lofty and profound thoughts of God's infinite resources. There rang in His heart the assurance, 'I am El Shaddai' (the God Who is enough).

It is remarkable that, throughout Abraham's life, God was continually giving new glimpses into His own glorious nature. With every temptation, call to obedience, or demand for sacrifice, a new and deeper revelation was entwined. This fed his faith and gave it unstaggering strength. Child of God, feed thy faith on Promise. For every look at your difficulties, take ten at what thy God is."—*Rev. F. B. Meyer, D.D.*

"Standing on the promises that cannot fail,
When the howling storms of doubt and fear assail
By the living Word of God I shall prevail,
Standing on the promises of God.

Standing on the promises of Christ the Lord,
Bound to Him eternally by Love's strong cord,
Overcoming daily with the Spirit's sword,
Standing on the promises of God."

A GENUINE FAITH

"Be of good cheer: for I believe God, that it shall be even as it was told me"—Acts xxvii.25.

"PAUL was strong because he believed. Faith makes men strong. When mistaken there is a power in faith for mischief; for good if the right thing is believed. Paul's faith was faith in God. 'I believe God.' That was something more than saying 'I believe *in* God.' This many do, but derive but slender comfort. But 'I believe God', believe Him, believe His truthfulness, His mercy, His power. This made Paul calm, peaceful, strong. Believing God, he believed God's message and was revived by it. He was sure that no hair of any man's head would be harmed. And he did that when there was nothing else to believe in. . . . It is a grand thing to believe God when the winds are out. The common run of men's faith is fair-weather faith. . . . Genuine faith in God speaks out and says, 'God is true, and I will stake everything on His word.' "

Rev. C. H. Spurgeon.

"Trust Him when dark doubts assail thee,
Trust Him when thy strength is small;
Trust Him, when, to simply trust Him
Is the hardest thing of all.

Trust Him! He is ever faithful;
Trust Him! for His will is best;
Trust Him! for the heart of Jesus
Is the only place of rest.

Trust Him, then, through cloud and sunshine,
All thy cares upon Him cast;
Till the storms of life are over,
And the trusting days are past."

(*Lucy A. Bennett.*)

ONLY BELIEVE !

To behold the miraculous.

"He . . . hangeth the earth upon nothing."—Job xxvi. 7.

IN looking to God for deliverance of any kind, we are prone to try to discover what material He has on hand to work on, in coming to our relief. If we are praying for financial help, we are apt to look over the community to see if we can think of anyone whom the Lord might influence to lend us some money. If there are no apparent probabilities in that direction, we find it difficult to believe for hard cash. . . . It is so human to look and crave for something in sight that will help the Lord out. In time of need, if we can only find a little something for God to begin on, we seem so much better satisfied. To need a sum of money and not be able to think of a friend, a man, or a monied institution, from which it might be obtained, gives a dark background to the scene . . . The outlook is all liabilities, with no resources to help out.

Now, to God's child what is the real situation ? Is there nothing but liabilities ? Much every way. Are there no resources ? Yes, thousands, millions, billions, trillions ! Where are they ? Earth and air are full of wealth untold. Can't you see it ? You do not need to see it. *Keep your eye on Him.* Just think a moment. It is not necessary for you to see any help in sight, nor is it really necessary for God to have any relief on hand. He does not need anything to begin on. In the beginning God created the heaven and the earth. What did He make them out of ? Nothing, absolutely nothing. When the earth was made, what did He hang it on ? Nothing. Pretty satisfactory earth to be made of nothing, eh ? Remember, not a scrap of anything was used to make it ! 'He . . . hangeth the earth upon nothing.' It hangs all right, doesn't it. Very well, then. A God Who can make an earth, a sun, a moon, and stars out of nothing, and keep them hanging on nothing, can supply all your needs, whether He has anything to begin to work with or not. Wonderful, isn't it ? Trust Him, and He will see you through. He has to make all your supplies out of nothing."—*P.J.S.*

" I smiled to think God's greatness
Lay around my incompleteness,
And around my restlessness—His rest."

INCOMPATIBLE THINGS

"Casting all your care upon Him; for He careth for you" ("It matters to Him about you")—I Peter v.7.

"THERE are two things which are more utterly incompatible than even oil and water, and these two are trust and worry. Would you call it trust, if you should give something into the hands of a friend to attend to for you, and then should spend your nights and days in anxious thought and worry as to whether it would be rightly and successfully done? And can you call it trust, when you have given the saving and keeping of your soul into the hands of the Lord, if day after day, and night after night, you are spending hours of anxious thought and questionings about the matter? When a believer really trusts about anything, he ceases to worry about that thing which he has trusted. And, when he worries, it is a plain proof that he does not trust. Tested by this rule, how little real trust there is in the Church of Christ! No wonder our Lord asked the pathetic question, 'When the Son of Man cometh shall He find faith on the earth?' He will find plenty of activity, a great deal of earnestness, and doubtless many consecrated hearts; but shall He find *faith*—the one thing He values more than all the rest? It is a solemn question, and I would that every Christian heart would ponder it well."

H.W.S., in "The Christian's Secret of a Happy Life".

"Is there any cross or trial?
  Tell it. Leave it.
Is there call for self-denial?
  Tell it. Leave it.
Is there suffering or pain?
  Tell it. Leave it.
Oft-times in our loss there's gain.
  Tell it. Leave it.

Jesus knows—*He has the care*—
Need I then the burden share?
Telling, leaving, thou shalt find—
Peace and rest with joy combined."

(***Bessie Jarvis.***)

ONLY BELIEVE !

To find peace when dying.

" If the Son shall make you free, ye shall be free indeed."—John viii. 34-36.

" AH, atheism, agnosticism, scepticism, unbelief, are miserably unsatisfying, despite the brag and bombast so often associated with them. The spiritual and intellectual nature of man cannot be satisfied with mere negations, blank denials, unanswered questionings, and blind, deaf, dumb, *helpless unbelief*. The soul of man cries out for positive truth,—and finds it in Jesus Christ. Atheism fails in the crises of life, and in the solemn hour of death. A little girl lay dying. Her mother was a Christian and had sent the little mite to Sunday School, and here she had learned to love Jesus. The father was a rank atheist. The little girl said: 'Daddy, I'm dying: whose religion shall I have, yours or mother's?' The atheist father hung his head, and then said shamefacedly: 'I think you'd better have mother's.' The real truth about atheism, as Dr. Torrey used to say, is that men hope, by the *denial of God's existence*, to shield themselves from the *discomfort of God's acknowledged presence*.

'The battle is on the will.' . . . In the great majority of cases the intellect is already on the side of Christian truth, and the heart is drawn by the appeal of the Saviour's love, but the will fights against making a definite decision for Christ. At this very moment Christ stands ready to save. He *died* to save! He *rose* to save! He *lives* to save! He *longs* to save! He is able to save to the uttermost—from the *penalty* and the *pollution* and the *power* of sin; and, finally, at His Second Coming, from the *presence* of sin. What a Saviour! What a salvation! The biggest sin of all sins is to harden the will against this matchless Gospel of Divine grace. The battle is on the will! The battle is on the will! Shall the Victory be for Christ?"—*Rev. J. Sidlow Baxter.*

" I yield! I yield!
I can hold out no more;
I sink, by dying love compelled,
And own Thee Conqueror!"